THIS WALKER BOOK BELONGS TO:

Wendy Howard-Williams

First published 1984
by Walker Books Ltd
87 Vauxhall Walk
London SE11 5HJ
as *jangle twang*

This edition published 1989

© 1984, 1989 John Burningham

Printed in Italy by Grafedit S.p.A.

British Library Cataloguing in Publication Data
Burningham, John
A grand band
I. Title
823'.914[J]   PZ7
ISBN 0-7445-1303-0

A GRAND BAND

John Burningham

WALKER BOOKS
LONDON

When I boom upon my drum,
Bear booms along with me;
We both go booming down the street,
And people come to see.

But when I play my bagpipes,
The bear, he seldom hears;
He stays a long, long way behind
And covers up his ears.

The piano is an instrument
He'll listen to for ages;
It helps a lot if while I'm playing,
The bear will turn the pages.

And if I play a jolly jig,
The bear is very glad;
But the fiddle has some other sounds
Which make him really sad.

When I slide on my trombone,
It makes a blaring sound;
And while Bear is conducting,
I can knock him to the ground.

I clash the cymbals very loud,
They make a mighty din;
The bear is not expecting it
And jumps out of his skin.

When I play the clarinet,
(I'm really not that good),
Bear listens very patiently,
Which I don't think he should.

And if I'm twanging on my harp,
Bear likes to twang as well;
But by the sound his twanging makes,
He's dreadful! You can tell!

To play the double bass is good;
Bear tries to dance – I wish he could!
Instead he bounces up and down –
I think he looks just like a clown.

I tinkle on the triangle,
The sound it does not vary,
Then he prances round and round
And looks just like a fairy.

We like to sway, the two of us,
To the maracas' sound;
I'm told they first came from Brazil,
It's there they can be found.

And when I strum on my guitar,
The songs of Spain and France,
The bear he loves to twirl about,
He's proving he can dance!

Another thing he likes to do
Involves the tambourine:
He likes to dance holding a rose!
It really should be seen.

It's when I play the trumpet,
Bear really goes quite barmy;
He wants us both to march about
And thinks we're in the army.

But when I toot upon my flute,
The bear becomes inspired:
He'll leap about and whoop and shout –
He makes me feel quite tired.

And when we've played with everything,
Sometimes we'll simply stand and sing;
Bear says if *he* must make a choice,
It really has to be – THE VOICE!

MORE WALKER PAPERBACKS

THE PRE-SCHOOL YEARS

John Satchwell
& Katy Sleight
Monster Maths
ODD ONE OUT   BIG AND LITTLE
COUNTING   SHAPES

FOR THE VERY YOUNG

Byron Barton
TRAINS   TRUCKS   BOATS
AEROPLANES

PICTURE BOOKS
For All Ages

Colin West
"HELLO, GREAT BIG BULLFROG!"
"PARDON?" SAID THE GIRAFFE
"HAVE YOU SEEN THE CROCODILE?"
"NOT ME," SAID THE MONKEY

Bob Graham
THE RED WOOLLEN BLANKET

Russell Hoban
& Colin McNaughton
The Hungry Three
THEY CAME FROM AARGH!
THE GREAT FRUIT GUM ROBBERY

Jill Murphy
FIVE MINUTES' PEACE

Philippa Pearce
& John Lawrence
EMILY'S OWN ELEPHANT

David Lloyd
& Charlotte Voake
THE RIDICULOUS STORY OF
GAMMER GURTON'S NEEDLE

Nicola Bayley
Copycats
SPIDER CAT   PARROT CAT
POLAR BEAR CAT   ELEPHANT CAT
CRAB CAT

Michael Rosen
& Quentin Blake
Scrapbooks
SMELLY JELLY SMELLY JELLY
(THE SEASIDE BOOK)
HARD-BOILED LEGS
(THE BREAKFAST BOOK)
SPOLLYOLLYDIDDLYTIDDLYITIS
(THE DOCTOR'S BOOK)
UNDER THE BED
(THE BEDTIME BOOK)

Jan Ormerod
THE STORY OF CHICKEN LICKEN

Bamber Gascoigne
& Joseph Wright
BOOK OF AMAZING FACTS 1

Martin Handford
WHERE'S WALLY?